Discover & Learn

Ancient Greeks

This book is perfect for pupils studying the Ancient Greeks in KS2 History (ages 7-11).

It's packed with facts, sources and questions covering the daily life, achievements and legacy of the Ancient Greeks — perfect for exploring and understanding the whole topic.

Published by CGP

Contributor: John Davis

Editors: Tom Carney, Catherine Heygate, Katya Parkes, Gabrielle Richardson

ISBN: 978 1 78294 967 1

With thanks to Alex Fairer, Maxine Petrie and Hannah Roscoe for the proofreading.

With thanks to Jan Greenway for the copyright research.

Printed by Elanders Ltd, Newcastle upon Tyne

Clipart from Corel®

Photocopying more than one section of this book is not permitted, even if you have a CLA licence.

Extra copies are available from CGP • 0800 1712 712 • www.cgpbooks.co.uk

Contents

Section One — Introduction to Ancient Greece

Welcome to Greece 2

Meet the Ancient Greeks 4

Athens vs Sparta 6

Section Two — Daily Life in Ancient Greece

The Greeks at Home 8

Growing Up in Greece 10

Women in Greece 12

Farming, Fishing and Food 14

Clothes and Beauty 16

The Olympic Games 18

Section Three — Ancient Greek Culture

Ancient Greek Beliefs 20

Greek Myths 22

The Theatre 24

Artistic Achievements 26

Science and Philosophy 28

Section Four — The Greeks at War

Warfare 30

Alexander the Great 32

Section Five — The Legacy of Ancient Greece

Lasting Achievements 34

Section Six — Glossary

Glossary 36

Welcome to Greece

Greece, known to its inhabitants as 'Hellas', has a rich and fascinating past. Historians and archaeologists study Ancient Greece today by visiting old cities to excavate and explore the remaining ruins. Items found in these places can tell us a lot about Ancient Greek life.

Grecian geography

Greece is made up of a mainland connected to Europe and thousands of islands (only about 200 have people living on them today).

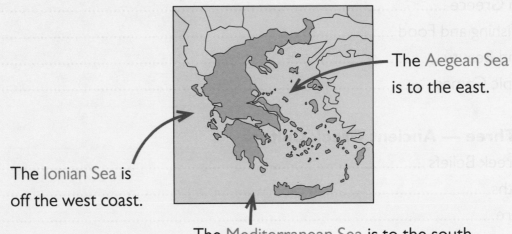

The Aegean Sea is to the east.

The Ionian Sea is off the west coast.

The Mediterranean Sea is to the south.

The lay of the land

About 80% of the land in Greece is mountainous. This made it difficult for the Ancient Greeks to farm crops or travel overland. However, Greece has around 8500 miles of coastline, so the Greeks were able to use the sea for much of their transport.

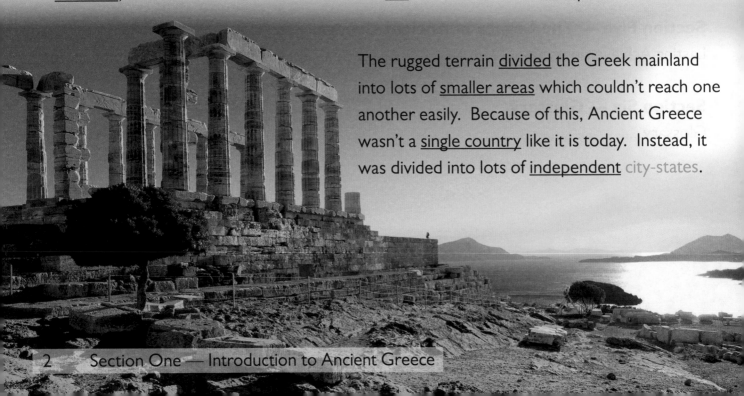

The rugged terrain divided the Greek mainland into lots of smaller areas which couldn't reach one another easily. Because of this, Ancient Greece wasn't a single country like it is today. Instead, it was divided into lots of independent city-states.

What a state

City-states were areas of land in Ancient Greece made up of a main city and the surrounding countryside. Each city-state was separate from the others and had its own way of life, but they all shared the same language and beliefs.

Most city-states developed near the coast so they could use the sea for food and to trade. The main city-states included Thebes, Corinth, Argos, Sparta and Athens.

How do you know?

We know about life in Ancient Greece from surviving buildings and art, as well as discoveries at ancient sites. Ancient Greek vases like the one on the left were often painted with scenes from daily life. These paintings can tell us about how the Ancient Greeks lived.

How else might we learn about life in Ancient Greece?

In 1876, a German archaeologist called Heinrich Schliemann excavated Mycenae. He found lots of gold treasures, including the mask on the right. He thought it was the funeral mask of the legendary Greek King Agamemnon, who is believed to have taken the Mycenaeans to war against Troy.

Not so fast...

Handling evidence isn't always easy, and archaeologists sometimes get things wrong. Modern archaeologists now think that Schliemann's mask was made hundreds of years before King Agamemnon lived.

It's important for archaeologists to think carefully about any evidence so they can work out what it is, where it's from, and how it can teach us about the past.

Rock on

The Ancient Greeks were up against it from the start, but a tough landscape didn't stop them from becoming a hugely impressive civilisation. Now, let's get introduced properly...

Meet the Ancient Greeks

Greek civilisation started around 3000 BC with the <u>Minoans</u>. They were followed by the <u>Mycenaeans</u>, before Greece entered its '<u>Dark Age</u>', a period we know very little about. From 800 BC onwards though, Ancient Greece rapidly became an <u>incredible civilisation</u>.

Island dwellers

<u>Minoan</u> civilisation existed on the <u>large island</u> of Crete between about 3000 BC and 1400 BC. The Minoans grew crops in the rich soil and <u>traded</u> to become wealthy. They built <u>decorative</u> <u>palaces</u> like this one at Knossos. It's thought that <u>invaders</u> or a <u>volcanic eruption</u> led to the decline of their civilisation.

Timeline

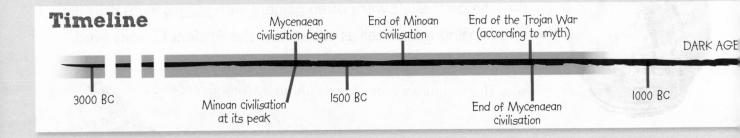

Mycenaean civilisation begins

End of Minoan civilisation

End of the Trojan War (according to myth)

DARK AGE

3000 BC

Minoan civilisation at its peak

1500 BC

End of Mycenaean civilisation

1000 BC

Mighty Mycenaeans

The <u>Mycenaeans</u> (1600-1200 BC), a <u>warlike</u> and strong people, ruled several Greek cities, including a <u>walled city</u> called Mycenae. Some historians call them the 'first Greeks' because they spoke a very early form of the Greek language.

Do you think modern Greek people would be able to talk to the Mycenaeans? Why?

In Greek legend, it was the Mycenaeans who conquered Troy (page 30). Their own city was well defended by huge stone walls. The main entrance was the '<u>Lion Gate</u>' — a large gateway with a sculpture of two lions on top. Despite these defences, it's thought that they may have been defeated by foreign <u>invaders</u>.

Dark days

The period between the collapse of the Mycenaean civilisation and about 800 BC is known as the <u>Greek Dark Age</u>. During this time, the Mycenaean language was <u>lost</u>, so there are no written sources. <u>Very little art</u> was produced either. This means that archaeologists find it <u>hard to learn more</u> about the Dark Age.

Why do you think some modern archaeologists call this period of time the 'Dark Age' of Greece?

By the 9th century BC, Greek civilisation had started to <u>regrow</u>. We can tell this because more art started being produced, like this vase from Athens.

First Olympic Games

Homer writes Iliad and Odyssey

500 BC

Battle of Marathon

Socrates dies

Alexander the Great dies

Romans take over Greece

AD 1

First modern Olympic Games

Today

The best of times

As the Dark Age came to an end, city-states developed all over Greece and became increasingly rich and powerful. <u>Rivalries</u> sprang up between some city-states, especially between <u>Athens</u> and Sparta.

By the 5th century BC, <u>Athens</u> was becoming a dominant power in Greece, and Athenians were making <u>amazing advances</u> in art, architecture, philosophy, medicine, the sciences and theatre.

Unfortunately, this didn't last. A <u>war</u> between <u>Athens</u> and <u>Sparta</u> had a huge impact on the city-states and made it easier for Macedonia to conquer Greece. Greece was later taken over by <u>Rome</u>.

Times gone by

If this quick stroll through the history of Ancient Greece hasn't filled you up with facts, don't worry — there's plenty more Greek goodness waiting on the pages ahead...

Athens vs Sparta

In 479 BC, the two most <u>powerful</u> city-states, Athens and Sparta, <u>teamed up</u> to defeat the Persians, but their friendship didn't last long. Less than 50 years later, they were at war.

Athenian success

At the start of the 5th century BC, Athens only ruled a small region of Greece. However, after leading the Greek states to <u>victory</u> against Persia in 479 BC, the Athenians took control of a large group of city-states. This made Athens the most powerful city in Ancient Greece.

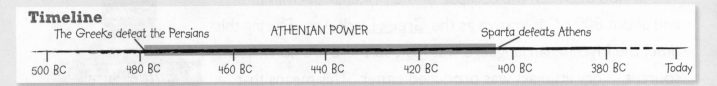

Pericles, an Athenian military leader and politician, was key to the city's <u>success</u> in the 5th century BC. He also built lots of new temples in Athens, including the Parthenon, which still stands on a hill above Athens today.

The picture below shows what the Parthenon might have looked like when it was built.

The Athenians loved art and literature, and they wrote lots of famous books during the 5th century BC. This means that Athens is <u>really important</u> to <u>historians</u> — most of their information about Ancient Greece comes from these Athenian sources.

Power to the people

Athens developed a new system of government called democracy. Under this system, ordinary citizens were able to vote on military decisions and changes to the law. All male citizens were expected to attend the assembly, a meeting where they voted by putting their hands up.

Women, foreigners and slaves were banned from attending the assembly, so they didn't get a vote.

Do you think Athenian democracy was a fair way of running the state?

Spartan revenge

Before Athens rose to power, Sparta had been one of the most powerful city-states in Greece. However, as Athens became more powerful, tensions with Sparta began to grow. Things came to a head in 431 BC, when war broke out between Athens and Sparta.

Pericles knew that the Athenian army was no match for the Spartans. Whenever Sparta attacked, he ordered the Athenians to stay inside the city walls. This meant that the war dragged on for 27 years until Sparta built a huge navy and won by attacking Athens from the sea.

Very little writing exists from Sparta. This means that a lot of what we know about Sparta comes from Athenian sources.

Why might we not trust Athenians writing about Sparta?

The Golden Age of Athens?

Fifth-century BC Athens is sometimes called 'the Golden Age of Athens', because of its artistic and military success. That all ended after the city's defeat by Sparta though.

The Greeks at Home

The weather in Greece is often warm and sunny, so Ancient Greek houses were designed to keep the people living in them cool.

Mud houses

Houses in Ancient Greece were usually quite <u>simple</u>. They were normally built out of <u>mud bricks</u> because these were <u>strong</u> and easy to make.

Mud bricks aren't long-lasting, so no Greek houses built from them survive today. However, some houses in the ruined city of Olynthus were built on <u>stone</u> foundations, which are <u>still intact</u>. These show us how Greek houses were <u>laid out</u>.

Rooms of the house

Greek homes were usually built around a courtyard, which helped to keep the house <u>cool</u>. Around the courtyard were many of the same rooms that we have in modern houses. Ancient Greek houses had <u>windows</u>, but they didn't contain glass — <u>wooden shutters</u> kept the sun out. The picture below shows what a rich family's house might have looked like.

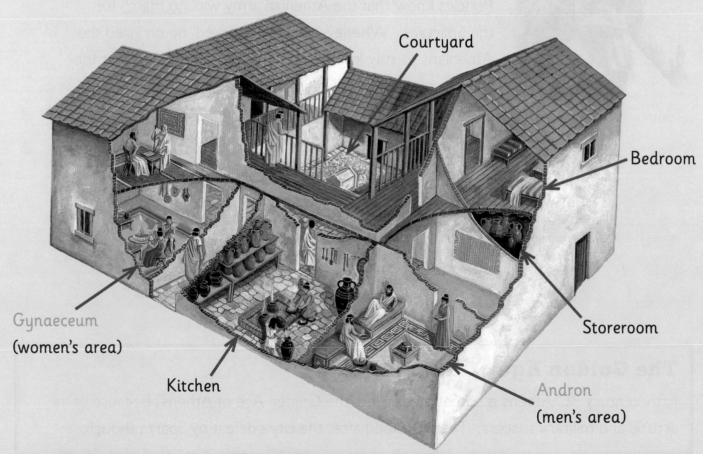

Courtyard

Bedroom

Gynaeceum
(women's area)

Storeroom

Kitchen

Andron
(men's area)

Home comforts

Greek women were expected to avoid public places (page 12), so they spent much of their time at home. Many wealthy Greek households had separate areas for men and women. The women's living area was called the gynaeceum. In here, women would manage daily household tasks like weaving and looking after their children.

The men's area was called the andron. It was often beautifully decorated, with an intricate mosaic on the floor and elaborate furniture, including couches for men to lie on during drinking parties. The andron sometimes had a separate entrance so male guests wouldn't bump into any women who lived in the house when they were visiting.

Do you think that the Ancient Greeks saw men and women as equal? Why or why not?

Bathtime

Most Ancient Greek homes didn't have a bathroom. Some rich women had slaves who fetched water so they could have baths at home, but most people bathed in the nearest stream. There were also public baths, where anyone could go to wash with warm water.

The Ancient Greeks didn't have flushing toilets. Instead, people used chamber pots, then emptied them into the street.

What problems could using chamber pots cause?

This picture shows a chamber pot which would probably have been used by an Ancient Greek child.

There's no place like home

Although the Ancient Greeks built their houses from simple materials, they were quite similar to our houses today. I wouldn't want to live somewhere without a toilet though...

Growing Up in Greece

Greek children had a tough start in life. When they were born, their father might decide not to keep them — sickly children were often <u>abandoned</u>. Ancient Greek families hoped for male children, because boys were considered <u>more valuable</u>. A girl couldn't carry on the family name, and her family had to give her husband money when she got married.

Do you think rich or poor Greeks were more likely to abandon their babies? Why do you think this might have been?

Playtime

Childhood in Ancient Greece wasn't all doom and gloom. We would recognise many of the games Greek children played, including <u>blind man's buff</u>. Like modern children, the Ancient Greeks also played with <u>toys</u>. Rattles, spinning tops, dolls, pull-toys and marbles were all enjoyed in Ancient Greece.

This toy horse probably once had string through its nose so that its owner could pull it along.

Greek children played with <u>pottery</u> figures. This pig was used as a rattle.

Knuckling down

This model shows two women playing a game called <u>knucklebones</u>. This involved throwing and catching small bones in a skilful way. The <u>bones</u> came from sheep's ankles! A version of the game (jacks) is <u>still played</u> today, but sheep's bones are no longer used.

Not all fun and games

Only <u>boys</u> went to <u>school</u> in Athens — <u>girls</u> were educated <u>at home</u>. Boys could only go to school if their parents could afford it. They started school at the age of seven and were taught to <u>read</u>, <u>write</u> and <u>count</u>.

Fitness was very important in Ancient Athens. Boys were taught <u>physical education</u> in a gymnasium. Another key part of a boy's education was <u>music</u>. This piece of pottery shows a boy being taught how to play the flute.

Do you think an Athenian education would prepare you for life in the modern world?

Spartan school

<u>All</u> Spartan boys, rich or poor, went to a school called an agoge. Here, they were trained to be <u>fit</u> and <u>loyal</u> <u>soldiers</u>. Training was <u>intense</u>, and boys were taught to withstand great pain. They were given <u>little food</u> and were expected to steal more when they got hungry.

If Spartan boys were found with stolen food, they were <u>punished</u> — <u>not</u> for <u>stealing</u> but for <u>getting caught</u>.

<u>Girls</u> had a <u>better education</u> in Sparta than elsewhere in Greece. They were encouraged to <u>exercise</u> and stay healthy — they could practise racing, wrestling and horse-riding. The Spartans believed that this would help their women produce <u>stronger babies</u> who would grow up to become <u>tough soldiers</u>.

Athenian subjects weren't that different from ours...

...but I don't fancy Spartan school. Wherever they were, Greek children really had their work cut out for them. Athenian boys faced tricky lessons, but the Spartans had gruelling physical exercises to do. At least there were still plenty of toys to play with...

Women in Greece

Women in Ancient Greece didn't have much freedom — most of them were completely dependent on their husbands. Spartan women were slightly better off, but not much.

Family life

Girls in Ancient Athens often married by their early teens, usually to an <u>older man</u> who might be more than twice their age. Married women managed the <u>household</u> and brought up <u>children</u>.

Athenian women couldn't vote, own land or inherit property. They couldn't have jobs and were often expected to <u>avoid</u> public areas. They weren't allowed to mix with men outside of their family.

<u>Poor women</u> had <u>more freedom</u> than rich ones. Doing <u>chores</u> like fetching water and shopping allowed them to see their friends. <u>Rich women</u> had <u>slaves</u> to do these jobs, so they <u>rarely</u> left the house.

Would you have preferred to be a rich woman or a poor woman in Ancient Greece? Why?

Priestess power

Becoming a priestess was one of the only ways a Greek woman could get to a position of power. In fact, the high priestess of the goddess <u>Athena</u> was the most important religious figure in Athens.

The Oracle at Delphi was the most <u>famous</u> priestess in Greece. The Ancient Greeks believed that she had <u>visions</u> of the <u>future</u>. They went to her for advice before making important military decisions.

Influential women

We don't know that much about women in Ancient Greece. Hardly any of the surviving sources were written by women, and women are rarely mentioned in sources written by men. However, there were some it was hard to ignore.

Sappho was a famous <u>poet</u> from Lesbos. She is one of the few female poets we know about from Ancient Greece. The Greeks admired her <u>love poetry</u>, but most of it is now lost.

Aspasia was the partner of the Athenian general Pericles and gave him <u>political advice</u>. Her wisdom was highly <u>respected</u> by the philosopher Socrates (page 28).

Sporting heroines

Spartan women had more <u>rights</u> than women in Athens — they could inherit and own property. They also <u>married later</u>, between the ages of <u>18 and 20</u>. While their husbands were <u>training</u> for war, Spartan women took charge of the family <u>finances</u> and ran the family farm.

Spartan women were encouraged to take up <u>sports</u>. The Spartan woman in this statue is wearing a short running skirt. It is very <u>different</u> from the clothes worn by Athenian women, who were expected to <u>cover up</u>.

What do you think the Athenians might have thought of Spartan women?

It's a man's world...

Women in Ancient Athens couldn't do lots of the things that men could. Spartan women had a slightly better deal — when the men went to war, they were in charge.

Farming, Fishing and Food

Only about <u>one-fifth</u> of the land in Greece is <u>suitable</u> for <u>farming</u> — the rest is <u>too rocky</u>. The rainfall in Greece is also <u>unreliable</u>, which can <u>stop</u> crops from <u>growing</u> well. Because of this, the Ancient Greeks had to <u>work hard</u> to make sure they had enough food.

Growing pains

It's estimated that up to <u>80%</u> of people worked in <u>food production</u>. Most farms were small and farmers only had <u>basic equipment</u> — they didn't even have <u>spades</u>. Most work was done by hand, although richer farmers had oxen to help them <u>plough</u> their fields.

Five a day

<u>Fruit trees</u> grow well in Greece, so fruit formed a large part of the Ancient Greek diet — <u>figs</u> and <u>raisins</u> were popular. They were often used to <u>sweeten</u> food, as the Greeks didn't have sugar.

Olives were popular too. In Athens, it was believed that the olive tree was a <u>gift</u> from the goddess <u>Athena</u> (page 20). It was a <u>crime</u> to tear down an olive tree there.

The Ancient Greeks believed that garlic would help make you strong, so Olympic athletes (pages 18-19) ate lots of it.

Daily bread

Women would grind grains like barley and wheat <u>at home</u> to make porridge or bread. The Ancient Greeks seem to have really loved bread — it's thought that they had <u>more than 60 different kinds</u>.

Meat and fish

Many Ancient Greek families kept a few sheep or goats to provide <u>milk</u> for <u>cheese</u>. The Greeks didn't eat very much meat. It was usually only eaten on <u>special occasions</u>, when an animal was sacrificed to the gods.

Greece is ideal for <u>fishing</u>, as it is almost <u>surrounded</u> by the <u>sea</u>. This meant that both <u>rich</u> and <u>poor</u> people in Ancient Greece ate a lot of <u>fish</u>. They often cooked their fish with herbs or dipped it into a sauce.

> Would you have enjoyed eating like an Ancient Greek? Why or why not?

Wine not?

The warm Greek climate is ideal for growing <u>grapes</u>, which the Greeks used to make their favourite drink — wine. The Greeks would crush the grapes with their <u>feet</u>, collecting the juice in barrels. The Greeks always mixed their wine with <u>water</u> before drinking it.

<u>Wine</u> was an important part of Ancient Greek symposia. These were <u>after-dinner</u> drinking <u>parties</u> where men were entertained by music or poetry. As well as having serious discussions, they also played a game called <u>kottabos</u> where competitors had to try and flick small amounts of wine at a target.

This is making me hungry...

The food of the Ancient Greeks wasn't that different from what people in Greece eat today. Bread, olive oil, goat's cheese and fish are all still popular in modern Greece.

Clothes and Beauty

Beauty was incredibly important to the Ancient Greeks. Their art often shows elegant people in graceful poses, and they decorated themselves with bright clothing and jewellery.

Bodies of art

Keeping fit and looking after your body was important if you wanted to be a good soldier or athlete in Ancient Greece. Sculptures and paintings on vases tell us how the Ancient Greeks thought people should look. They often show young and healthy Greeks, so we know healthy bodies were considered beautiful.

The men painted on this ancient vase are competing in a running race. They are all strong and muscular, like the ideal Greek.

That's a wrap

In early Ancient Greece, women wore a long tunic called a peplos. Later, they began wearing a different kind of tunic called a chiton, which was also worn by men. This was fastened at the shoulders and belted at the waist.

Both men and women wore a cloak called a himation, which was often wrapped over one shoulder. Thin cloaks were worn in summer, and thicker ones were made for winter.

Do you think you would be comfortable in Ancient Greek clothes? Why?

Clothes could be brightly coloured or white. They were usually made of flax or wool and often had to be produced at home.

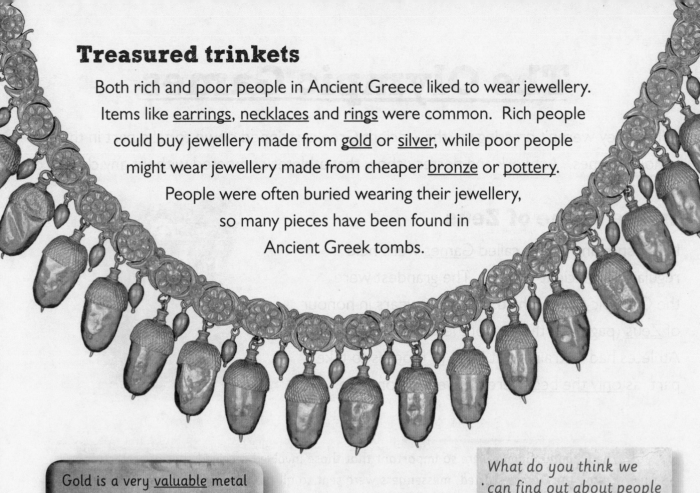

Treasured trinkets

Both rich and poor people in Ancient Greece liked to wear jewellery.
Items like <u>earrings</u>, <u>necklaces</u> and <u>rings</u> were common. Rich people
could buy jewellery made from <u>gold</u> or <u>silver</u>, while poor people
might wear jewellery made from cheaper <u>bronze</u> or <u>pottery</u>.
People were often buried wearing their jewellery,
so many pieces have been found in
Ancient Greek tombs.

> Gold is a very <u>valuable</u> metal
> because it's quite <u>rare</u> and it
> <u>doesn't rust</u> or lose its shine.

> What do you think we
> can find out about people
> by studying the jewellery
> they were buried with?

Naturally beautiful

To keep their appearance tip-top, the Ancient Greeks used many <u>natural products</u>.
For example, both men and women used <u>olive oil</u> as a <u>moisturiser</u> for their skin.

Having <u>pale skin</u> was fashionable in Ancient Greece — it showed that you were
wealthy and didn't have to work outside in the sun. To make their skin look pale,
Greek women put <u>white lead</u> on their faces. We now know that this material is <u>toxic</u>!

Many Ancient Greeks thought that make-up shouldn't
be too <u>obvious</u>, but women did <u>colour</u> their lips and cheeks
with make-up made from <u>fruits</u>, like mulberries. For a time, it
was fashionable to have connected eyebrows ('a <u>unibrow</u>').

It's all in the eye of the beholder

With their inventive (if dangerous) cosmetics, it's clear that the Ancient Greeks really did
care about their appearance. They tried incredibly hard to stay healthy and beautiful.

The Olympic Games

When they weren't dressing up, the Ancient Greeks stripped down to take part in their famous Games. Artwork and pottery show that athletes competed without any clothes on.

In the name of Zeus

Major sporting events called <u>Games</u> were held regularly in Ancient Greece. The grandest were the Olympic Games, held every four years in honour of <u>Zeus</u> (page 20), the king of the Greek gods. Athletes had to train for at least <u>10 months</u> to take part, as <u>only the best</u> were allowed to compete.

The Olympic Games were so important that those involved received special protection. Before the Games started, messengers were sent to all the Greek <u>city-states</u> ordering them to allow athletes and spectators to travel to the Games safely.

Let the games begin

The first Olympic Games are thought to have been held at Olympia in <u>776 BC</u>. A running race called the stadion was the only event for the first 13 Olympics. Eventually, the Olympic Games became a <u>major five-day festival</u> with a whole host of events including chariot racing, wrestling, long jumping, javelin, discus, boxing and running races in full armour.

Which of the Olympic events listed above do you think you'd be best at?

Classic vs Modern

The final ancient Olympics were held in AD 393 after 293 Games spanning over 1000 years. In 1896, the Games were brought back in a modern format which still continues today. These 'new' Olympic Games have some similarities and differences to the original ones:

Similarities

- Cheating was severely punished. The punishments were a bit different though — ancient athletes who were caught cheating could be flogged.

- Athletes raced in trials before a final race between the best of the best to find the overall champion.

Differences

- People were less worried about the athletes' safety. Men sometimes died in the boxing events and horse racing was more dangerous than it is today.

- The fastest times were not recorded. The goal was to be the best that year, not to beat previous records.

Only men could compete in the ancient Olympic Games, but unmarried women were allowed to watch the events. Married women were forbidden from even watching the Games — they risked being thrown off a cliff if they were caught spectating.

Crowning glories

Originally, the greatest achievement at the Olympic Games was to win the stadion. The athlete who won this event would have been famous all across Ancient Greece.

The overall winner of each event was awarded a kotinos. This was a crown made from sacred olive leaves (page 14), and athletes who won one were greatly admired.

Ahead of the game

The Olympic Games were a pretty big deal in Ancient Greece. Winners were like modern sports stars — they would be famous throughout Greece. Their events were a lot more dangerous than today's though. I definitely wouldn't fancy taking part...

Ancient Greek Beliefs

Religious beliefs were central to people's lives in Ancient Greece. The Greeks believed that the gods controlled the world, so they worshipped them and tried to keep them happy.

Gods on Earth

The Ancient Greeks believed in <u>many different gods</u> and <u>goddesses</u>. Every god was believed to be responsible for a different part of life. Greek people would pray to different gods depending on the kind of help that they needed.

The gods were believed to be immortal and have <u>supernatural powers</u>, but according to Greek myths, they also fell in love, <u>had children</u>, fought and argued — just like humans.

The gods were said to live on Mount Olympus in Greece.

A family affair

Of all the Greek gods, <u>Zeus</u> was the <u>most powerful</u>. He <u>ruled</u> the rest of the gods from his throne on Mount Olympus. The rest of the gods were members of Zeus's family. <u>Athena</u>, the goddess who gave her name to Athens, was a <u>daughter of Zeus</u>. Athena was believed to have been <u>born</u> from <u>Zeus's head</u> after Zeus asked Hephaestus to <u>cut it open</u> with an axe.

Gods of Olympus

Zeus — king of the gods
Hera — queen of the gods
Poseidon — god of the sea
Athena — goddess of wisdom
Ares — god of war
Apollo — god of music and light
Artemis — goddess of the moon
Aphrodite — goddess of love
Hephaestus — god of fire
Dionysus — god of wine and theatre
Hermes — messenger of the gods
Demeter — goddess of farming

Every city in Ancient Greece held its own religious festivals throughout the year. The rest of the time, people worshipped at temples or at altars in their homes.

One of the greatest temples was the <u>Temple of Apollo</u> at Delphi — its ruins can still be seen today. Greeks believed this holy site was the <u>centre of the world</u>. It contained a theatre, a stadium and about <u>20 treasuries</u> to hold <u>gifts</u> that people brought for Apollo.

Judgement day

The Ancient Greeks believed that the dead went to an <u>underworld</u> below the ground which was ruled by Zeus's brother, the god <u>Hades</u>. This underworld was thought to be surrounded by <u>rivers</u>. To reach it, you had to pay <u>Charon</u>, the ferryman, to take you across on his boat. People were often buried with <u>coins</u> to pay Charon so that their souls wouldn't be stranded between life and death.

This picture shows Hades on his throne in the underworld.

Say your prayers...

The Ancient Greek gods were well respected, although people didn't believe they had to live a 'good life' to make them happy. People did expect harsh punishments if they made any of the gods angry though — so many stayed on their best behaviour just in case.

Greek Myths

The Ancient Greeks had lots of traditional stories about past heroes and their adventures with gods and monsters. These stories were incredibly popular — many are still told today.

There's a myth for that

The Ancient Greeks used myths to <u>explain</u> everything around them. One myth told how humans were taught to make <u>fire</u> by a Titan called <u>Prometheus</u>. Another myth explained how the <u>sky</u> was <u>held up</u> by a Titan called <u>Atlas</u>.

Natural events were also explained with myths. <u>Earthquakes</u> were said to be caused by the god <u>Poseidon</u> (page 20) crashing his trident to the ground, and it was thought that the <u>seasons changed</u> when <u>Persephone</u>, the goddess of spring, went to and from the underworld every <u>six months</u>.

Why do you think the Ancient Greeks used myths to explain things? Can you think of any myths that you've been told to explain something?

Is everyone listening?

<u>Homer</u> lived during the 8th century BC. He wrote two famous poems about the <u>Trojan War</u> and how a <u>hero</u> called <u>Odysseus</u> struggled to get home afterwards.

These myths were a good source of <u>entertainment</u>. They were passed on by <u>word-of-mouth</u> (like stories told around a campfire), so even people who <u>couldn't read</u> could enjoy them.

Myths let the Ancient Greeks <u>remember</u> their ancestors as heroes who travelled far and fought dangerous battles. Whether or not the stories were <u>true</u> wasn't that important — <u>connecting with the past</u> and <u>enjoying</u> listening were the real aims.

A wing and a prayer...

Myths could contain <u>warnings</u>. In one myth, <u>Icarus</u> and his father <u>Daedalus</u> were imprisoned by the King of Crete. To escape, Daedalus made <u>wings</u> by sticking <u>feathers</u> to a frame with <u>wax</u>. The two began flying to safety with their new wings, but Icarus became overexcited. He ignored his father's advice and flew closer and <u>closer to the sun</u>. The sun <u>melted</u> the wax on <u>Icarus's wings</u> and he fell to his death.

What do you think people learnt from the myth of Icarus?

The myth of <u>King Midas</u> is also a <u>warning</u>. Midas was granted his wish that <u>everything he touched</u> turned to <u>gold</u>. He soon discovered that this <u>stopped</u> him from <u>eating</u> and <u>drinking</u>, and he even turned his daughter into a statue. He begged to have the wish undone and stopped being so greedy.

Heroic Heracles

Other myths featured <u>heroes</u> like <u>Heracles</u>, the son of Zeus. These myths gave the Ancient Greeks role models who demonstrated things like <u>courage</u> and <u>determination</u>.

Heracles was told to complete <u>12</u> seemingly <u>impossible</u> <u>tasks</u>, including killing a giant lion, slaying a nine-headed monster and stealing a herd of man-eating wild horses.

After Heracles succeeded in all of the tasks, he was given immortality and joined the gods on Mount Olympus.

Stories with significance

The Ancient Greeks were natural storytellers. Lots of their most exciting myths are still told today, with many having been adapted for TV or film. For the Greeks though, these myths were not just stories — they were a link to their past and a guide for the future.

The Theatre

The Ancient Greeks invented theatre as we know it. From heart-breaking tragedies to side-splitting comedies, many of the plays they wrote are still performed onstage today.

Making a play for it

Plays became popular in Ancient Greece in the 6th century BC. It's thought that early plays were inspired by the rituals that were carried out to worship Dionysus, the god of wine (page 20) — these involved wearing masks, singing and sacrificing goats!

When plays took off, the Theatre of Dionysus was cut into the southern cliff face of the Acropolis in Athens. There were competitions to see who could write the best play, and the winning writers and actors earned prizes and fame — just like modern film stars.

Setting the stage

Theatres in Ancient Greece were large, open-air spaces, carved into natural slopes. This allowed tiered seating to be built, which gave everyone a good view of the stage. The design of the theatre helped sound to carry well, so people at the back could hear the actors' voices. Actors would stand in front of a skene, a small tent or building at the back of the stage, often painted to look like the play's setting.

The modern word 'scene' comes from the Greek word 'skene'.

The theatre at Epidaurus could hold around 14 000 spectators at once.

Express yourself

The Ancient Greeks had <u>two main types</u> of play: <u>tragedies</u>, which saw a <u>hero</u> suffer a <u>terrible fate</u>; and <u>comedies</u>, which were often about <u>ordinary people's lives</u> and contained lots of <u>rude jokes</u>.

<u>Only men</u> were allowed to <u>act</u> and there could only be <u>three actors</u> <u>onstage</u> at once. Actors played several different characters, so they wore <u>masks</u> to help the audience tell them apart. The masks had <u>large expressions</u> which could be seen from the <u>back</u> of the theatre.

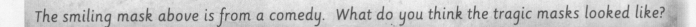

The smiling mask above is from a comedy. What do you think the tragic masks looked like?

King of the quill

It is believed that <u>Sophocles</u> (496-406 BC) entered <u>30 competitions</u> and <u>won 24</u> of them. He is thought to have written about <u>120 plays</u> in total, though only seven have survived to the present day.

His best-known play is called <u>Oedipus the King</u>. It is a tragedy about Oedipus, a man who accidentally <u>kills his father</u> and <u>blinds</u> <u>himself</u> after his <u>mother dies</u> — not a happy story at all!

In the play, Oedipus solves the <u>riddle</u> of the Sphinx:
"What creature walks on four legs in the morning,
two legs at noon and three in the evening?"

*Can you work out the answer to this legendary riddle?**

The show must go on...

We have a lot to thank the Ancient Greeks for — without their invention of acting and the theatre, cinema and television as we know them today would not exist. Their creative skills didn't stop there though. Turn over to discover what else kept them busy...

Artistic Achievements

Ancient Greece was <u>famous</u> for its architecture. The Ancient Greeks built grand temples with huge stone columns — a style that has been <u>copied</u> by many modern architects. The Greeks were also well known for their beautiful <u>painted pottery</u> and <u>lifelike statues</u>.

Seriously stylish

The grandest buildings in Greek cities were <u>temples</u> (page 21). These were usually large, rectangular buildings propped up by magnificent stone <u>columns</u> and decorated with beautiful <u>carvings</u> of leaves or flowers.

The <u>Temple of Hephaestus</u> in Athens was built in around 450 BC. It's the <u>best-preserved</u> ancient temple in Greece.

How did they do it?

Big chunks of <u>limestone</u> and <u>marble</u> were transported to building sites on carts. They were then carved into <u>elaborate shapes</u> with <u>hammers</u> and <u>chisels</u>, before being carefully lifted into place using <u>ropes</u> and <u>pulleys</u>.

Balancing act

The Ancient Greeks usually made columns by <u>stacking</u> <u>several blocks</u> of stone on top of each other. This made them very <u>stable</u> during <u>earthquakes</u> because each block could <u>wobble</u> a bit without making the whole column fall down.

Columns were <u>carved</u> in several styles. <u>Doric</u> columns were plain, <u>Ionic</u> columns were lightly decorated, and <u>Corinthian</u> columns were very fancy. Some columns, called caryatids, were carved to look like <u>women</u>.

Pottering about

Greek vases weren't just ornaments, they almost always
had a <u>practical use</u>. Vases came in many shapes and sizes,
depending on what they were for. The vase on the right is
a <u>krater</u> — it was used to mix wine with water at symposia.

Greek vases were <u>beautifully decorated</u> by skilled painters.
The Greeks had a unique style of painting, illustrating their
vases with <u>red</u> or <u>black figures</u> in many different scenes.

Vases were often painted with scenes from <u>everyday life</u> or
with scenes from Greek myths. This vase shows the hero
<u>Theseus</u> killing the Minotaur, a half-man, half-bull <u>monster</u>
who lived deep inside a mysterious labyrinth on Crete.

Strike a pose

The Ancient Greeks made <u>statues</u> for many of the <u>same reasons</u> we do
— for memorials and gravestones, and to <u>decorate</u> buildings. Greek
statues were incredibly <u>detailed</u> and <u>lifelike</u>, and they were often naked.
The Ancient Greeks weren't embarrassed by nudity — they <u>celebrated</u>
the human body and wanted sculptures of it to look <u>perfect</u>.

Ancient Greek statues were made from <u>marble</u> or <u>bronze</u>.
The marble statues that survive today are <u>white</u>, but they
would originally have been <u>painted</u> in <u>bright colours</u>.

> Why do you think the surviving Greek statues are white?

Copycat columns

Greek art and architecture have had a lasting impact. Ever since the Romans, civilisations
all over the world have been copying them. In cities as far apart as Madrid, Melbourne
and Moscow, you can still find buildings whose style was influenced by the Greeks.

Science and Philosophy

The Greeks were very <u>advanced thinkers</u> who loved exploring the mysteries of the universe. They invented philosophy, which helped them think about <u>tricky questions</u> like 'what is the meaning of life?' Greek philosophers tested their ideas by <u>debating</u> and <u>discussing</u> them.

Atomic bombshell

Many Greek ideas and discoveries are still relevant and useful to us today. It was a Greek called <u>Democritus</u> who first suggested that atoms make up the universe.

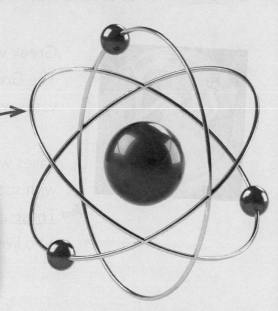

> A Greek geographer known as Eratosthenes calculated the distance around the Earth. Given that he didn't have any modern scientific equipment, his measurement was impressively close to the actual figure.

Three wise men

<u>Socrates</u> (469-399 BC) was declared the wisest man in the world by the Oracle (page 12). He thought it was important to question everything — even respected Greek <u>traditions</u>. This <u>upset</u> people, and he was eventually sentenced to <u>death</u> for not respecting the gods.

His student, <u>Plato</u>, founded the <u>Academy</u> in Athens, which became known as the <u>first university</u> in the western world. Plato's student <u>Aristotle</u> (384-322 BC) studied at the Academy for 20 years. His writings have influenced almost every field of human knowledge.

A medical marvel

This is a symbol of Asclepius.

Hippocrates (460-370 BC) was a Greek doctor. Some people call him the father of medicine. Before he came along, illnesses were seen as a punishment from the gods. People would pray to Asclepius, the Greek god of healing, for cures.

Hippocrates realised that illnesses weren't caused by the gods — he noticed that they had natural causes. He treated people's symptoms instead of praying for them to recover.

Do you think Hippocrates might have had a hard time convincing people that their illnesses hadn't come from the gods? Why?

Speaking volumes

Archimedes (287-212 BC) is one of the most famous Greek scientists. He discovered that you can use water to work out the volume of things. He noticed that when you put an object into a container full of water and let it sink to the bottom, the volume of water that spills out is the same as the volume of the object.

It's said that Archimedes made this discovery in his bathtub. The story goes that he was so excited with his find that he leapt up and ran through the streets without any clothes on!

You've got another think coming...

The Ancient Greeks really were geniuses. They came up with lots of ideas about life and the world that still hold true today. It wasn't always easy though — some free thinkers like Socrates were killed by enemies who didn't agree with their radical new ideas.

Warfare

The Greek city-states often attacked each other and had to defend against attacks in turn. Occasionally though, all of Greece would unite to fight off foreign invaders.

Hop to it

Boys trained as soldiers from the age of 18 in Athens and as young as 7 in Sparta (page 11). Most Greek soldiers were foot soldiers called hoplites. They fought in a formation called a phalanx — men lined up and used their shields to protect themselves and their neighbour. This made a long wall which faced the enemy. When Greek armies fought, it usually became a pushing match to see whose line would break first.

Why do you think the phalanx was so effective in battle?

At the battle of Thermopylae in 480 BC, the king of Sparta famously held off around 80 000 Persians for three days with just 7000 Greek hoplites. This was possible because the Greeks were fighting from a narrow mountain pass, so the Persians couldn't attack with their entire force. However, the Persians eventually found a hidden path around the Greeks and surrounded them.

One trick pony

The Greek myths include lots of stories about a war between the Ancient Greeks and the city of Troy. According to one story, the Greeks made a giant wooden horse and hid some soldiers inside. When they left the horse outside the walls of Troy, the Trojans brought the mysterious gift into the city. After nightfall, the Greek troops came out of the horse, opened the gates and let the rest of their army in — Troy had fallen.

Barge right in

Athens had a strong navy — at its peak it had up to 200 battle-ready warships called triremes. These were light wooden ships, about 35 metres long, with 170 oarsmen sitting on three levels on either side. They could reach speeds of up to 10 mph and had a bronze battering ram fitted at the front which could sink enemy boats.

Marathon men

In 490 BC, the Greeks defeated a Persian army at the Battle of Marathon. A Greek force of about 10 000 saw off around 20 000 Persians and chased them back to their boats. The Greeks then marched to Athens, arriving there before the Persian fleet, so they could defend the city against another attack. According to the Greek stories, 6400 Persians were killed while the Greeks lost just 192 men.

Do you believe the Greek figures for how many men were killed? Why?

The Ancient Greeks didn't shy away from a scrap...

...they fought often and well, using hoplite phalanxes and speedy warships to defeat their enemies. They still thanked the gods for their successes though — wars were avoided during religious festivals and sacrifices were made after great victories in battle.

Alexander the Great

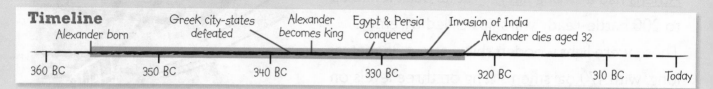

Timeline

Alexander born — Greek city-states defeated — Alexander becomes King — Egypt & Persia conquered — Invasion of India / Alexander dies aged 32

360 BC — 350 BC — 340 BC — 330 BC — 320 BC — 310 BC — Today

Alexander the Great was one of the <u>greatest military commanders</u> ever. He helped his father to conquer all of Greece and then went on to establish a huge empire.

Early life

Alexander was born in Macedonia in 356 BC. His father, King Philip II, was a successful war leader and Alexander learnt military skills from a young age. He also studied everything from biology to poetry with the famous philosopher <u>Aristotle</u> (page 28).

At just <u>12 years old</u>, Alexander <u>tamed</u> a mighty <u>horse</u> called <u>Bucephalus</u>. He later rode Bucephalus in many battles.

Empire building

In 338 BC, Alexander helped his father <u>defeat</u> the Greek city-states, giving Macedonia control of Greece. When his <u>father died</u> in 336 BC, Alexander became <u>king</u>. He gathered a great army and set off to <u>conquer</u> the <u>rest of the world</u>.

In 332 BC, Alexander defeated Syria and the island city of Tyre. Alexander then took control of Egypt, where he founded the city of Alexandria in 331 BC. Invading India in 326 BC, Alexander defeated <u>King Porus</u> whose army used <u>elephants</u> to charge at the attacking Greek forces.

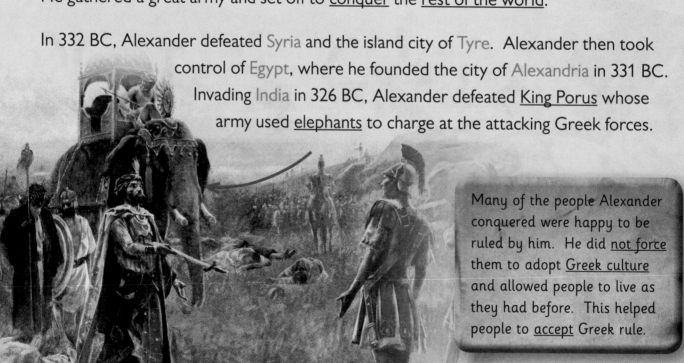

Many of the people Alexander conquered were happy to be ruled by him. He did <u>not force</u> them to adopt <u>Greek culture</u> and allowed people to live as they had before. This helped people to <u>accept</u> Greek rule.

The wars against Persia

Alexander faced the Persian armies of <u>King Darius III</u> several times. He defeated them at Issus in 333 BC, even though the Persian army was much larger. When the Persians started losing, King Darius <u>fled</u>, leaving his family behind.

Darius also <u>ran away</u> in 331 BC after Alexander defeated his army again, but he was later <u>killed</u> by one of his own men. The <u>Persian empire</u> now belonged to Alexander.

Knot a problem

According to legend, when Alexander marched into Gordium he found a wagon tied up with an impossibly <u>complicated knot</u>. A prophecy said that whoever undid it would become <u>ruler of Asia</u>. Alexander simply took his <u>sword</u> and <u>sliced</u> the <u>Gordian knot</u> in two.

Decline and fall

It wasn't all plain sailing for Alexander — his expansion into India was halted when his army <u>refused</u> to march any further away from their <u>homes</u> and <u>families</u>. Alexander agreed to his men's demands and returned west.

Unfortunately, Alexander never had the chance to go back to India. In June 323 BC, aged 32, Alexander died after suffering <u>ten days of fever</u>. His <u>empire</u> began to <u>crumble</u> as various people <u>fought</u> to replace him.

Lots of the surviving sources about Alexander were written by Greeks. Do you think these sources are likely to be accurate? Why or why not?

One of the greats

Alexander was no slouch. He created a huge, powerful empire (there's a map at the back of the book) and defeated enemies that often outnumbered him — all without ever losing a battle. Who knows how much greater he could have been if he'd lived a little longer...

Lasting Achievements

By 146 BC, the <u>Romans</u> controlled Greece. They were so impressed by Greek culture that they <u>adopted</u> Greek ideas and <u>spread</u> them across their empire — many still survive today.

A, B, G?

The word '<u>alphabet</u>' comes from the first two Greek letters, '<u>alpha</u>' and '<u>beta</u>'. Our alphabet was influenced by the Greek one, although ours has two extra letters. <u>Thousands</u> of our <u>words</u> come <u>from Greek</u> too, like 'geography', 'technology', and 'hexagon'.

A α Alpha	B β Beta	Γ γ Gamma	Δ δ Delta	E ε Epsilon	Z ζ Zeta
H η Eta	Θ θ Theta	I ι Iota	K κ Kappa	Λ λ Lambda	M μ Mu
N ν Nu	Ξ ξ Xi	O o Omicron	Π π Pi	P ρ Rho	Σ σ,ς Sigma
T τ Tau	Υ υ Upsilon	Φ φ Phi	X χ Chi	Ψ ψ Psi	Ω ω Omega

That's the spirit

The modern <u>Olympic Games</u> owe their existence to the Ancient Greeks (pages 18-19). In 2012, the <u>London Olympics</u> saw 10 000 athletes from 205 countries participate in 26 different sports, some of which were also practised at the ancient Games. The values of the ancient Olympics — <u>peace</u>, <u>excellence</u> and <u>healthy competition</u> — are still important to the Games today.

More power to you

The Greek system of democracy (page 7) went on to shape most modern governments and societies, including the UK's Houses of Parliament. <u>Improvements</u> have been made, such as giving <u>women</u> the right to <u>vote</u>, but the general idea of <u>people</u> having an active <u>say</u> in how their country is run can be traced back to Athens in the 5th century BC.

Drawing in the crowds

The Ancient Greeks' lifelike <u>sculptures</u> are still viewed in <u>museums</u> by <u>millions of people</u> every year. By creating models in <u>active poses</u>, the Greeks truly captured real life in their art.

Between 1801 and 1805, many ancient <u>carvings</u> were <u>taken</u> from the Parthenon and brought to Britain by <u>Lord Elgin</u>. Many of these carvings, sometimes called the <u>Elgin Marbles</u>, are still displayed in Britain. However, some people think they should never have been removed and want them to be <u>returned to Greece</u>.

Do you think the Elgin Marbles should be returned to Greece? Why?

Many ancient sculptures have been found <u>underwater</u>, especially those made of <u>bronze</u>. Because bronze is a <u>useful metal</u>, statues made from it were sometimes <u>melted down</u> to make <u>weapons</u> in times of war — sculptures lost underwater avoided this fate.

Classical architecture

The <u>elegant</u> architecture used by the Ancient Greeks to build temples and other <u>public buildings</u> (page 26) has inspired many later societies. In the UK, several important public buildings have been built in <u>imitation</u> of the classic Greek style.

Why do you think modern civilisations copied Ancient Greek architecture?

This photo shows the <u>British Museum</u> in London. The tall <u>columns</u> and ornate <u>roof carvings</u> were influenced by Ancient Greek buildings.

An enduring legacy

Long after its civilisation ended, Ancient Greece lives on. In our ways of thinking, our language, the buildings around us and the laws that govern our lives, Ancient Greece still shapes us today. It really makes you wonder how we'll be remembered in the future...

Glossary

acropolis	The central part of an Ancient Greek city, usually <u>on a hill</u>. The most famous acropolis was in <u>Athens</u>.
agoge	A <u>school</u> attended by all <u>male Spartans</u>. The agoge's difficult training made Spartan soldiers <u>loyal</u> and <u>strong</u> — they were considered the <u>greatest warriors</u> in Greece.
altar	The <u>table</u> where religious <u>rituals</u> and <u>sacrifices</u> were <u>performed</u>.
ancestor	A <u>family member</u> from <u>long ago</u> who someone is <u>descended</u> from.
andron	Part of an Ancient Greek <u>house</u> reserved for <u>men</u>. Used to <u>entertain male guests</u>.
archaeologist	A person who studies history by <u>digging up objects</u> and using them to find out more about the <u>past</u>.
architecture	The <u>style</u>, design or plan of a <u>building</u>.
atom	A <u>tiny particle</u> which is too <u>small</u> to see. Everything around you is made up of atoms.
caryatid	A <u>stone carving</u> of a <u>woman</u> used as a <u>column</u> to support <u>Greek buildings</u>.
chamber pot	A <u>bowl</u> in someone's house that is used as a <u>toilet</u>.
chariot	A <u>vehicle</u> pulled by <u>horses</u>. Used in <u>battle</u> and for <u>racing</u>.
city-state	A <u>city</u> and the area of <u>land</u> around it that together made up an <u>independent</u> state.
comedy	A type of <u>play</u>. In Ancient Greek theatre, comedies contained lots of <u>singing</u>, <u>dancing</u>, <u>witty conversation</u> and <u>rude jokes</u>.
courtyard	The <u>outside</u> area at the centre of most Greek <u>houses</u>.
democracy	A <u>system of government</u> where <u>ordinary people</u> get a say in how things are run. In Ancient Greece, <u>only men</u> were <u>allowed</u> to <u>vote</u>.
excavate	Carefully <u>digging</u> in an area to find buried <u>remains</u> or <u>ruins</u>.
flax	A crop grown to <u>provide food</u> or <u>make clothes</u>. <u>Linen</u> is a fabric made from the flax plant.
foundation	The <u>bottom layer</u> of a <u>building</u> which <u>supports</u> everything above it.
gymnasium	A Greek <u>building</u> used for <u>athletic activities</u>.
gynaeceum	The part of a house <u>reserved</u> for <u>women</u> in Ancient Greece.
hoplite	A heavily-armed <u>foot soldier</u> of Ancient Greece.

immortal	Having the ability to live forever.
labyrinth	A complicated network of passages. The Minotaur lived inside a labyrinth.
legend	A story that is set within human history, but which historians haven't been able to prove actually happened.
myth	A traditional story used by ancient societies to explain the world around them. They often involved gods and the supernatural.
Oracle	A priestess at Delphi who was thought to deliver visions of the future from Apollo.
oxen	The plural form of 'ox'. Male cattle, sometimes used by farmers to pull ploughs.
Parthenon	A temple on the Athenian Acropolis dedicated to the goddess Athena.
phalanx	An Ancient Greek battle formation. Soldiers stood side by side with their shields overlapping. This created one long shield wall.
philosophy	The study of knowledge. Philosophers ask difficult questions to try to gain a deeper understanding of the world around them.
politician	A person whose job is to help run a country's government. They may have the power to make or change laws.
priestess	A female religious leader. Few women held this position of power in Greece.
prophecy	A prediction of what will happen in the future.
Sphinx	In Greek mythology, the Sphinx was a creature with a human head, a lion's body and wings. It gave people riddles to solve, showing no mercy if they failed.
stadion	A running race in the ancient Olympics. The arena it took place in was also called a stadion.
symposia	Drinking parties held in Ancient Greece. Only men were allowed to attend.
symptom	A noticeable effect of an illness, such as a fever or a headache.
temple	A religious building dedicated to one or more gods.
Titan	Gigantic and powerful beings who were believed to have once ruled the universe. The Olympian gods are said to have defeated them in battle.
tragedy	A type of play. In Ancient Greek theatre, tragedies were usually about serious subjects like myths. Often, they featured a hero suffering a terrible fate.
trident	A spear with three points on it. The god of the sea, Poseidon, was often shown holding a trident.
volume	The amount of space that an object takes up.

Picture Acknowledgements

Cover photo: Chronicle / Alamy Stock Photo

Section One — Introduction to Ancient Greece
p3 (mask) Nikos Pavlakis / Alamy Stock Photo. p5 (vase) Granger Historical Picture Archive / Alamy Stock Photo. p5 (Apollo) Nikos Pavlakis / Alamy Stock Photo. p6 (Pericles) Jiri Hubatka / Alamy Stock Photo. p6 (Parthenon) North Wind Picture Archives / Alamy Stock Photo. p7 (Athenian democracy) De Luan / Alamy Stock Photo. p7 (warrior) Rolf Richardson / Alamy Stock Photo.

Section Two — Daily Life in Ancient Greece
p8 (Olynthus) Hercules Milas / Alamy Stock Photo. p8 (Greek house) Universal Images Group North America LLC / Alamy Stock Photo. p9 (Greek women) National Geographic Creative / Alamy Stock Photo. p9 (chamber pot) © Sharon Mollerus. Licensed under the Creative Commons Attribution-Share Alike 2.0 Generic Licence. http://creativecommons.org/licenses/by-sa/2.0/. p10 (toy horse) Dimitris K. / Alamy Stock Photo. p10 (pig rattle) Pig rattle, c.400 BC (pottery), Greek, (4th century BC) / Private Collection / Photo © Christie's Images / Bridgeman Images. p10 (knucklebones) Granger Historical Picture Archive / Alamy Stock Photo. p11 (vase painting) gameover / Alamy Stock Photo. p11 (Spartan warrior) © Andrew Howat / Look and Learn. p12 (Greek women) North Wind Picture Archives / Alamy Stock Photo. p12 (the Oracle at Delphi) The Artchives / Alamy Stock Photo. p13 (Sappho) www.BibleLandPictures.com / Alamy Stock Photo. p13 (Aspasia) Lanmas / Alamy Stock Photo. p13 (Spartan woman) Ancient Art and Architecture / Alamy Stock Photo. p15 (symposium) Science History Images / Alamy Stock Photo. p16 (vase) Ancient Art and Architecture / Alamy Stock Photo. p16 (man and woman) Chronicle / Alamy Stock Photo. p17 (necklace) © Ashmolean Museum / Mary Evans. p18 (Zeus) Hercules Milas / Alamy Stock Photo. p18 (Olympic Games) Lanmas / Alamy Stock Photo. p19 (kotinos) Eleni Seitanidou / Alamy Stock Photo.

Section Three — Ancient Greek Culture
p20 (birth of Athena) The History Collection / Alamy Stock Photo. p21 (Temple of Apollo) Stefano Paterna / Alamy Stock Photo. p21 (Hades) Lebrecht Music & Arts / Alamy Stock Photo. p22 (Poseidon) Purestock / Alamy Stock Photo. p23 (Icarus and Daedalus) © The Mullan Collection / Mary Evans. p23 (Heracles) Azoor Photo / Alamy Stock Photo. p24 (Dionysus) PRISMA ARCHIVO / Alamy Stock Photo. p25 (theatre mask) Peter Horree / Alamy Stock Photo. p25 (Oedipus and the Sphinx) Granger Historical Picture Archive / Alamy Stock Photo. p27 (vase) Artokoloro Quint Lox Limited / Alamy Stock Photo. p27 (Theseus and the Minotaur) Juan Aunion / Alamy Stock Photo. p27 (statue) Cosmin-Constantin Sava / Alamy Stock Photo. p28 (Socrates) PRISMA ARCHIVO / Alamy Stock Photo. p29 (Archimedes) Science History Images / Alamy Stock Photo.

Section Four — The Greeks at War
p30 (hoplites) The History Collection / Alamy Stock Photo. p31 (trireme) Zoonar GmbH / Alamy Stock Photo. p31 (Battle of Marathon) North Wind Picture Archives / Alamy Stock Photo. p32 (Bucephalus) Chronicle / Alamy Stock Photo. p32 (King Porus) North Wind Picture Archives / Alamy Stock Photo. p33 (battle scene) INTERFOTO / Alamy Stock Photo. p33 (Gordian knot) Heritage Image Partnership Ltd / Alamy Stock Photo. p33 (Alexander the Great) Peter Horree / Alamy Stock Photo.

Section Five — The Legacy of Ancient Greece
p34 (Olympic flag) Gerry Yardy / Alamy Stock Photo. p35 (statue) Alex Ramsay / Alamy Stock Photo. p35 (British Museum) eye35.pix / Alamy Stock Photo.